Bible
Research
made
easy

Mark Water

W9-BSB-682

HENDRICKSON
PUBLISHERS

Bible Research made easy
Hendrickson Publishers, Inc.
P.O. Box 3473
Peabody,
Massachusetts
01961-3473

Copyright © 1999
John Hunt Publishing
Text copyright © 1999
Mark Water

ISBN 1-56563-110-2

Designed and
produced by
Tony Cantale
Graphics

First printing —
December 1999

Manufactured in
China

Unless otherwise
noted, Scripture quo-
tations are taken from:
AV, New King James,
New Living Trans-
lation, The Message,
Contemporary English
Version, New Century
Version, NIV, NASB,
J.B. Phillips NRSV

**New Revised
Standard Version**
New Revised Standard
Version Bible,
Anglicized Edition,
copyright ©1989,
1995. Division of
Christian Education of
the National Council of
the Churches of
Christ in the United
States of America, and
are used by permis-
sion. All rights
reserved.

**New Living
Translation**
Scripture quotations
marked (NLT) are
taken from the *Holy
Bible*, New Living
Translation, copyright
© 1996. Used by per-
mission of Tyndale
House Publishers,
Inc., Wheaton, Illinois
60189. All rights
reserved.

**New Century
Version**
Scriptures quoted
from *The Holy Bible,
New Century Version*,
copyright © 1987,
1988, 1991 by Word
Publishing, Nashville,
Tennessee 37214.
Used by permission.

**Contemporary
English Version**
The New Testament
of the Contemporary
English Version: ©
The American Bible
Society 1995. Pub-
lished by Thomas
Nelson Publishers
under license from
The American Bible
Society.

**New King James
Version**
Scriptures taken form
the New King James
Version: © 1979,
1980, 1982 by
Thomas Nelson, Inc.
Used by permission.
All rights reserved.

The Message
Scripture taken from
THE MESSAGE.
Copyright © by
Eugene H. Peterson,
1993, 1994, 1995.
Used by permission of
NavPress Publishing
Group.

J.B. Phillips
The New Testament
in Modern English,
translated by J.B.
Phillips, Revised
Edition, Copyright ©
J.B. Phillips, 1958,
1959, 1960, 1972,
Used by permission of
the Macmillan
Company. All rights
reserved.

Acknowledgements
pp. 12-13 Extract
taken from *The NIV
Study Bible*, Hodder &
Stoughton, 1987. The
NIV Concordance,
copyright © 1982,
1984, by The
Zondervan
Corporation.

pp. 14-15 Extract
taken from *The NIV
Study Bible*, Hodder &
Stoughton, 1987.
Color Time Lines,
copyright © 1985, by
The Zondervan
Corporation.

pp. 16-17 Extract
taken from *The NIV
Study Bible*, Hodder &
Stoughton, 1987.
Notes, copyright ©
1985, by The
Zondervan
Corporation.

Pp. 18-19 Extract
taken from *The NIV
Study Bible*, Hodder &
Stoughton, 1987. The
Center-Column Cross
Reference System,
copyright © 1984, by
The Zondervan
Corporation.

pp. 20-21 Extract
taken from *The
Thompson Chain -
Reference Study Bible
NIV*, .B. Kirkbride
Bible Co., Inc. 1990.

pp. 24-27 Extracts
taken from *The New
Strong's Exhaustive
concordance of the Bible*,
Thomas Nelson
Publishers, 1984

pp. 34-35 Extract
taken from *Vine's
Complete Expository
Dictionary of Old and
New Testament Words*,
W.E. Vine, William
White Jr., Merrill F.
Unger, ANG Pub.
1990.

pp 36-37 Extract taken
from *Easton's Bible
Dictionary*, M.G.
Easton, Nelson, 1991

pp 38-39 Extract taken
from *Nave's Topical
Bible*, Orville J. Nave,
Nelson, 1997

pp 40-41 Extract taken
from *The International
Bible Commentary*,
(General Editor, F.F.
Bruce), Zondervan,
1986

pp 42-43 Extract taken
from *The Message of
Acts*, John Stott, IVP,
1990

pp 44-45 Extract taken
from *The New Unger's
Bible Handbook*,
Revised by Gary N.
Larson, Moody Press,
1984

pp 46-47 Extract taken
from *The New
Dictionary of Theology*
(edited by S.B.
Ferguson and D.F.
Wright), IVP, 1988

Photography supplied
by Foxx Photos,
Goodshoot, Digital
Vision and Tony
Cantale

Illustrations by
Tony Cantale
Graphics

Contents

Special pull-out chart

Bible study on the Net

Introduction to Bible research

Research is ...

- If you copy what one other person has written it is called plagiarism;
- If you copy what two or more people have written it is called research!

Contemporary biblical research

A great deal of biblical research today focuses on finding something that is new, innovative or original.

This book does not approach Bible research in that way at all.

It's purpose is to show you how to use Bible reference books and to help you come to a clearer understanding of a given Bible text.

Bible reference tools

To receive benefit from this book no other book is necessary only a Study Bible (see pages 6-7). However, 13 other books which aid detailed Bible Study will be mentioned.

1. A Bible concordance (see pages 22-23)
2. Strong's **Exhaustive Concordance of the Bible** (see pages 24-27)
3. A Greek New Testament (see pages 28-29)
4. A Greek lexicon and a Hebrew lexicon (see pull outchart, section 5)
5. A Greek-English interlinear New Testament (see pages 32-33)
6. An expository dictionary of New Testament words (see pages 34-35)
7. A Bible dictionary (see pages 36-37)
8. A topical Bible (see pages 38-39)
9. A one volume Bible commentary (see pages 40-41)
10. A commentary on a specific book of the Bible (42-43)
11. A Bible handbook (44-45)
12. A Bible theology book (see pages 46-47)
13. A Bible atlas (see pages 48-49)

It is not necessary to have these reference books to study this book. In fact, if you do not own any of them, it may be best for you to finish reading this book before deciding which ones to buy. At that point you will be in a better position to choose the books that are most appropriate for you.

A lesson from Nehemiah

The aim of this book is summed up by the following words:

"The Levites ... instructed the people in the Law while the people were standing there. They read from the Book of the Law of God, making it clear and giving the meaning so that the people could understand what was being read. ... Then all the people went away ... to celebrate with great joy, because they now understood the words that had been known to them."
Nehemiah 8:7-8, 12

Start simple

What you need to make use of this book

- You will need a good Study Bible.
- If you don't know what a Study Bible is, a Christian bookstore will be able to show you a variety of them and demonstrate their unique features.
- With each of the major translations of the Bible, one or more Study Bibles are usually published.
- These Study Bibles are also often available in libraries.

(Unless otherwise stated, the Bible studies in this book are based on the *New International Version* of the Bible.)

Many of the topics in this book are treated on two levels.

simple start

The first level introduces the topic and suggests preliminary ways of studying the text. This will aid in understanding its meaning and allow God to speak directly to you. You will find this first level under the heading: **A simple start.**

SOLID BIBLE STUDY

The second level gives a more in-depth approach to a passage or subject. These second level studies come under the heading: **Solid Bible study.** They will suggest different avenues of Bible study which may take many months rather than a few minutes.

Pick and choose

Don't feel that you have to do *every* Bible study in this book.

Pick the studies that appeal to you and are most appropriate for your needs.

William Tyndale

When William Tyndale, the English Reformer and Bible translator, was imprisoned before he was eventually burnt at the stake, he made the following request.

> "A warmer cap, a candle, a piece of cloth to patch my leggings. ... But above all, I beseech and entreat your clemency to be urgent with the Procurer that he may kindly permit me to have my Hebrew Bible, Hebrew Grammar and Hebrew Dictionary, that I may spend time with them in study."

Do you love God with your mind?

> "Do your best to present yourself to God as one approved, a workman who does not need to be ashamed and who correctly handles the word of truth."
> *2 Timothy 2:15*

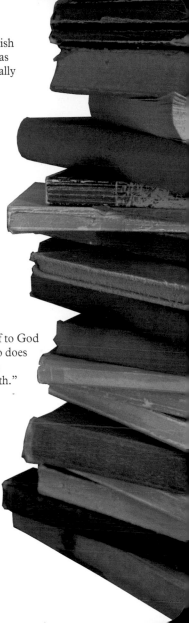

Choosing a Bible version

The best selection ever
Never before has there been such a good selection of trustworthy translations of the Bible to choose from.

King James Version: KJV
The *King James Version*, also known as the *Authorized Version*, is the oldest continuously published English translation of the Bible.

It was first published in 1611, at the suggestion of King James I of England, 1566-1625. It is loved for the beauty of its traditional English. But over the centuries the meaning of some English words has changed. Therefore this version does not always communicate understandably to readers today.

New International Version: NIV
The *New International Version* is a translation of the Bible produced by over 100 scholars working from the best available Hebrew, Aramaic and Greek texts. The goals of the translators were to produce an accurate translation that would have clarity and literary quality. The *NIV* had its beginning in 1965. The *NIV* New Testament was published in 1973, and the Old Testament was finished in 1978.

It is conservative in its theological position and accurate in its translation.

New Living Translation: NLT
The New Living Translation is a completely revised edition of *The Living Bible*. It has been recommended by Billy Graham for its "greater readability and accuracy."

The Living Bible: TLB
Published in 1971, Kenneth Taylor's single-author paraphrase is praised for its ability to communicate directly with the reader and for its theologically conservative stance. However, scholars have pointed out that some of the translator's own assumptions are evident and that some parts are very loosely translated. *The Living Bible* is often given to people who are unfamiliar with the Bible to help them more easily understand it.

The Message
Designed for reading rather than for study, *The Message* is a unique, idiomatic, contemporary rendering of the Bible text in modern language by Eugene Peterson. It is helpful for devotional reading and for clarifying difficult passages.

New American Standard Bible: NASB

55 conservative scholars, using the insights of modern scholarship, produced this translation in 1971 to replace the *American Standard Version* of 1901. While preserving the literal accuracy of the 1901 *ASV*, the *NASB* has sought to render grammar and terminology in contemporary English. Special attention has been given to the rendering of verb tenses to give the English reader a rendering as close as possible to the sense of the original Greek and Hebrew texts.

The New American Standard Bible 1995 edition is an updated version of this word-for-word translation.

New King James Version: NKJV

The New King James Version was produced by 130 evangelical scholars in 1982. It is an updated version of the *King James Version*.

The New Revised Standard Version: NRSV

The *NRSV* is based on the *Revised Standard Version*, published in 1952, which, in turn, aimed to replace the *American Standard Version*, of 1901. The *RSV* used modern scholarship but included an occasional liberal bias. The language of the *NRSV* is modern, yet dignified, reflecting the long tradition of translation with which it is associated, that started with the 1611 *King James Version* of the Bible

Contemporary English Version: CEV

The *CEV*, which was released in 1994, was written for people who want an accurate contemporary English rendering of the Bible that remains thoroughly readable. It endeavors to put the precise meaning of the original languages into words that clearly communicate. The *CEV* was translated directly from the Greek text published by the United Bible Societies (third edition, corrected, 1983).

Questions to ask

When you choose to read or buy a Bible version, either for yourself, or for somebody else, ask:

• Is it a paraphrase or a translation?
• Is it to be used to gain a speedy acquaintance with the general meaning of the text, or is it for detailed study?
• Is it for children or for adults?
• Is there a school grade readability level associated with this version?

Comparison of eight Bible versions

The Contemporary Parallel New Testament

This is a parallel Bible, which contains in its 1,840 pages, the full text of the New Testament in the classic King James Version and in seven of the modern English translations:

- New King James Version
- New Living Translation
- The Message
- Contemporary English Version
- New Century Version
- New International Version
- New American Standard Bible

2 Corinthians 7:10

As you read this verse in different Bible versions, note the differences and what they teach about the word "repentance." Can you understand the origin of repentance?

King James Version: "For godly sorrow worketh repentance to salvation not to be repented of: but the sorrow of the world worketh death."

New King James Version: "For godly sorrow produces repentance (leading) to salvation, not to be regretted, but the sorrow of the world produces death."

New Living Translation: "For God can use sorrow in our lives to help us turn away from sin and seek salvation. We should never regret this kind of sorrow. But sorrow without repentance is the kind that results in death."

The Message: "Distress that drives us to God does that. It turns us around. It gets us back in the way of salvation. We never regret that kind of pain. But those who let distress drive them away from God are full of regrets, end up on a deathbed of regrets."

Contemporary English Version: "When God makes you feel sorry enough to turn to him and be save, you don't have anything to feel bad about. But when the world makes you feel sorry, it can cause your death."

New Century Version: "The kind of sorrow God wants makes people change their hearts and lives. This leads to salvation, and you cannot be sorry for that. But

Bible sales in the USA

| New Living Translation 4% |
| Living Bible 1.5% |
| New Revised Standard Version 1.5% |
| Other 2% |
| New International Version 48% |

the kind of sorrow the world has brings death."

New International Version: "Godly sorrow brings repentance that leads to salvation and leaves no regret, but worldly sorrow brings death."

New American Standard Bible: "For the sorrow that is according to the will of God produces a repentance without regret, leading to salvation, (or, leading to a salvation without regret) but the sorrow of the world produces death."

Making up your own eight versions

Of course, you don't have to stick to the eight versions in *The Contemporary Parallel New Testament*. You can choose other versions for additional comparisons.

Comparing only four translations would greatly increase your appreciation of the text of the New Testament. In order to supersede the effectiveness of this way of studying you would need to have a good knowledge of the original languages.

In the J.B. Phillips paraphrase one of the most memorable translations is of the first part of Romans 12:2: "Don't let the world around you squeeze you into its own mold." Compare this with the translations found in the *Contemporary Parallel New Testament* below:

King James Version: "And do not be conformed to this world."

New King James Version: "And do not be conformed to this world."

New Living Translation: "Don't copy the behavior and customs of this world."

The Message: "Don't become so well-adjusted to your culture that you fit into it without even thinking."

Contemporary English Version: "Don't be like the people of this world."

New Century Version: "Do not change yourselves to be like the people of this world."

New International Version: "Do not conform any longer to the pattern of this world."

New American Standard Version: "And do not be conformed to this world."

SOLID BIBLE STUDY

Investigate the ways different Bible versions translate key New Testament passages, such as John 1:1-18; Philippians 2:1-11; Colossians 2:1-10.

Features of a Study Bible –
Character studies

People
Many Study Bibles provide a listing of the names of people mentioned in the Bible. (The studies on pages 12-15 are correct for *The New International Version* and may differ slightly in other translations.)

SOLID
BIBLE STUDY

Make a study of all the references in the New Testament about the twelve apostles and so build up your own character sketch of each of them.

Identifying the important people
Some lists identify the important people by giving a one, or two, line summary of their lives. For example, under the letter B, from among the many of names

Balaam
Prophet who attempted to curse Israel (Nu 22-24; Dt 23:4-5; 2 Pe 2:15; Jude 11). Killed in Israel's vengeance on Midianites (Nu 31:8; Jos 13:22).

Balak
Moabite king who hired Balaam to curse Israel (Nu 22-24; Jos 24:9).

Barnabas*
Disciple, originally Joseph (Ac 4:36), prophet (Ac 13:1), apostles (Ac 9:27), Antioch (Ac 11:22-29; Gal 2:1-13), on the first missionary journey (Ac 13-14). Together at Jerusalem Council, they separated over John Mark (Ac 15). Later co-workers (1 Co 9:6; Col 4:10).

the following might be singled out. Key Bible verses are supplied.

People marked with an asterisk (*) indicate that every appearance of that person in the Bible is listed.

Bartholomew*
Apostle (Mt 10:3; Mk 3:18; Lk 6:14; Ac 1:13). Possibly also known as Nathanael (Jn 1:45-49; 21:2).

Baruch
Jeremiah's secretary (Jer 32:12-16; 36; 43:1-6; 45:1-2).

Benjamin
Twelfth son of Jacob by Rachel (Ge 35:16-24; 46:19-21; 1 Ch 2;2). Jacob refused to send him to Egypt, but relented (Ge 42-45). Tribe of blessed (Ge 49:27; Dt 33:12), numbered (Nu 1:37; 26:41), allotted land (Jos 18:11-28; Eze 48:23), failed to fully possess (Jdg 1:21), nearly obliterated (Jdg 20-21), sided with Ish-Bosheth (2 Sa 2), but turned to David (1 Ch 12:2, 29). 12,000 from (Rev 7:8).

Features of a Study Bible –
Chronological timelines

Timelines

Study Bibles often furnish useful information about Bible events and Bible people in the form of a chronological timeline.

These timelines offer a bird's eye view of historical events. They can also show how events recorded in the Bible relate to events which were going on in the world.

So, at the time of Jesus' birth, a New Testament timeline points out that the rulers in Palestine were under the control of the Roman Emperors.

Chronology of the Bible

Most Study Bibles provide charts giving an overview of the whole Bible. These charts attempt to date the events recorded in the Bible and position them in relation to when each Bible book was written.

You need to realize, though, that there is uncertainty about some of the dates. For example, no one is certain exactly when the book of Job was written. Some think it may have been the first Bible book written while others date it up to two thousand years later.

Certain dates continue to be hotly debated.

John the Baptist starts his ministry
AD 26

Jesus starts his ministry
AD 26

Jesus baptized
AD 26

John the Baptist imprisoned
AD 27

John the Baptist beheaded
AD 28

Jesus crucified AD 30

Jesus ascends
AD 30

Roman Procurator Pontius Pilate
AD 26-36

Herod the Great
37-4 BC

20 BC

10 BC

Jesus born
6/5 BC

Roman Emperor
Augustus
27 BC – AD 14

0

**Jesus in
the temple**
AD 6/7

**Roman
procurators
rule Palestine
from**
AD 6/7

AD 10

AD 20

The chronology (below) of the life of Jesus should be viewed with this in mind. Many scholars believe that the dating used to determine Christ's birth was erroneous. Hence, Jesus may have been born earlier than originally calculated, placing his birth at 5 or 6 BC. Once that is understood, it then means that Jesus' boyhood visit to the temple is placed twelve years later, at AD 6 or 7. When one date is fixed it determines many of the other dates, and, of course, if the original date is wrong, the other days will not be accurate.

SOLID
BIBLE STUDY

Read Matthew 21:1 –27:66; Mark 11:1 –15:47; Luke 19:28–23:56; John 12:12 –19:42, and construct your own chronology of the last week of Jesus' life. What have you learned from this?

Using study notes from a Study Bible

What are study notes?

Most Study Bibles include interpretative notes which are inserted throughout the Bible. These notes provide a commentary about the Bible text. They normally appear at the bottom of the page and look like extended footnotes.

The following commentary notes are taken from the *NIV Study Bible*.

1. Study notes explain concepts and important words

The study note on Matthew 3:2, "Repent, for the kingdom of God is near," reads:

3:2 **Repent**. Make a radical change in one's life as a whole. **the kingdom of heaven**. A phrase found only in Matthew, where it occurs 33 times. ... The kingdom of heaven is the rule of God and is both a present reality and a future hope. The idea of God's kingdom is central to Jesus' teaching and is mentioned 50 times in Matthew alone.

2. Study notes interpret verses which appear to contain difficulties

Did Jesus teach that we should hate our families?

The study note on Luke 14:26, "If anyone comes to me and does not hate his father and mother, his wife and children, his brothers and sisters - yes, even his own life - he cannot be my disciple" reads:

14:26 **hate his father**. A vivid hyperbole, meaning that someone must love Jesus even more than his immediate family (see Mal 1:2-3 for another use of the figure). See Mt 10:37.

3. Study notes link Bible events and Bible people

Moses is seen as a mediator.

The study note on Exodus 32:30, "Moses said to the people,

'You have committed a great sin. But now I will go up to the Lord; perhaps I can make atonement for your sin.'" reads:

32:30 make atonement for your sin. By making urgent intercession before God, as the mediator God had appointed between himself and Israel. No sacrifice that Israel or Moses might bring could atone for this sin. But Moses so identified himself with Israel that he made his own death the condition of God's destruction of the nations (see v. 32). Jesus Christ, the great Mediator, offered himself on the cross to make atonement for his people.

4. Study notes provide background information to shed light on a particular practice

Was there a moral question about eating meat sacrificed to animals?

The study note on 1 Corinthians 8:1, "Now about food sacrificed to idols" reads:

8:1 Now about food. Another matter the Corinthians had written about. **sacrificed to idols**. Offered on pagan altars. Meat left over from a sacrifice might be eaten by the priests, eaten by the offerer and his friends at a feast in the temple or sold in the public meat market. Some Christians felt that if they ate such meat, they participated in pagan worship and thus compromised their testimony for Christ. Other Christians did not feel this way.

5. Study notes show how one passage illuminates another passage

The study notes on Psalm 26:8, "I love the house where you live, O Lord, the place where your glory dwells," reads:

26:8 where your glory dwells. The presence of God's glory signaled the presence of God himself: (see Exodus 24:16; 33:22.) His glory dwelling in the tabernacle (see Ex 40:35), and later this temple (see 1 Ki 8:11), assured Israel of the Lord's holy, yet gracious, presence among them. John 1:14 announces that same presence in the Word become flesh who "made his dwelling among us".

SOLID BIBLE STUDY

Read through an unfamiliar book of the Bible and read through the accompanying commentary notes from a Study Bible.

Using a Bible cross reference

Raised numbers or letters

Study Bibles have tiny raised numbers or letters accompanying some of the words in most of the Bible verses.

These letters/numbers are similar to footnotes in a book. They lead you to a matching letter/number which is either at the foot of the page or in a column in the center of the page.

Following the letter/number is a cross-reference to another verse on a similar topic in the Bible.

You need eagle eyes to see the cross references

Look up Genesis 1:1. Following the word "beginning" is a tiny raised letter ᵃ.

In the margin, or at the foot of the page you will find the figure **1**. This indicates which verse numbers the cross references link to. As you look at the first verse of Genesis chapter one, you will see **1**ᵃ Ps 102:25.

The compilers of these cross references thought that it would be a good idea for us to look up Psalm 102, verse 25 in connection with the word "beginning" in Genesis 1:1

"In the beginning you laid the foundations of the earth, and the heavens are the work of your hands." *Psalm 102:25.*

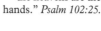

Using cross-references

Use your Bible to look up the cross-references listed below for the first verse of the Bible.

When you come across the abbreviation "ver" in the cross references it means you are to look up a verse from the chapter that you are studying. So the first one you will find reads "ver 21" – you then look up and read Genesis 1, verse 21.

At the front of your Study Bible you will find a list of abbreviations used for books of the Bible.
Ps denotes Psalms, **Isa** denotes Isaiah, etc.

Genesis 1:1

Bible text	Cross references
In the beginning^a	**1** ^a Ps 102:25; Pr 8:23; Isa 40:21; 41:4, 26; Jn 1:1-2
God created^b	^b ver 21, 27; Ge 2:3
the heavens^c	^c ver 6; Ne 9:6; Job 9:8; 37:18; Ps 96:5; 104:2; 115:15; 121:2; 136:5; Isa 40:22; 42:5; 51:13; Jer 10:12; 51:15
and the earth.^d	^d Ge 14:19; 2 Ki 19:15; Ne 9:6; Job 38:4; Ps 90:2; 136:6; 146:6; Is 37:16; 40:28; 42:5; 44:24; 45:12, 18; Jer 27:5; 32:17; Ac 14:15; 17:24; Eph 3:9; Col 1:16; Heb 3:4; 11:3; Rev 4:11; 10:6

As you search these verses you may find yourself following your own train of thought. Add your own references in the margin.

SOLID
BIBLE STUDY

Look up all the cross references in the letter of Jude.

Make a note of the way your study will hopefully change your behavior or affect your attitude to a problem.

Using a Bible chain reference

The purpose of chain references

The chain reference system helps you learn from the links between occurrences of particular words in the Bible. The word may show you how it is used in a particular Bible book. The word may show you how different writers used the same word at different times.

How the chains work

In a chain reference Bible the text of certain words are highlighted in **bold**.

These words are found in the margin of the Bible and are in alphabetical order.

Following the bold word, Bible references are given to other places in the Bible where the word occurs.

In the following example from 2 Corinthians in *The Thompson Chain-reference Study Bible*, *NIV* there are a number of features to note about the notes in the margin.

- **Pilot number**: The "Pilot Number" in the numerical system–at the left of the topics on the margin–leads directly to the same topic in the Comprehensive Helps section where all references are found.
- **Forward reference in chain**: The reference at the right of the topic is the "Forward Reference" which leads to the end of the "chain." One obtains each reference in its Scriptural setting by following a "chain."

The symbol † indicates the end of a "chain". Parallel passages are marked (p.p.) in the margin.

BIBLE STUDY

Follow through the use of the word "turn" in Mark's and Luke's gospels in a Bible chain reference Bible. Note how the word is used in different ways.

Sometimes it refers directly to repentance, sometimes it illustrates what repentance is and sometimes it uses the word "turn" in other ways.

7 Since we have these promises, dear friends, let us purify ourselves from everything that contaminates body and spirit, perfecting holiness out of reverence for God.

Paul's joy

²Make room for us in your hearts. We have wronged no one, we have corrupted no one, we have exploited no one. ³I do not say this to condemn you; I have said before that you have such a place in our hearts that we would live or die with you. ⁴I have great confidence in you; I take great pride in you. I am greatly encouraged; in all our troubles my joy knows no bounds.

⁵For when we came into Macedonia, this body of ours had no rest, but we were harassed at every turn—conflicts on the outside, fears within. ⁶But God, who comforts the downcast, comforted us by the coming of Titus, ⁷and not only by his coming but also by the comfort you had given him. He told us about your longing for me, your deep sorrow, your ardent concern for me, so that my joy was greater than ever.

⁸Even If I caused you sorrow by my lett... not regret it. Thou did regret it—I see my letter hurt you, only for a little w ⁹yet now I am happy because you were sorry, but because sorrow led you to r tance. For you b sorrowful as God i ed and so wer harmed in any way ¹⁰Godly sorrow repentance that le salvation and lea regret, but worl row brings deat what this godly has produced what earnestnes eagerness to cle selves, what ind what alarm, wh ing, what conce readiness to se done. At every have proved y to be innocen matter. ¹²So ev I wrote to yo snot on acco one who did or of the inj but rather t God you co yourselves h to us you are. we are encou

In additio encourageme especially see how hap because his refreshed b

Using a Bible concordance

Using a Bible concordance

A concordance is an index of all the major or key words in the Bible along with their immediate contexts. With a concordance you find the specific word you are looking for. The various places where that word occurs are listed in order from Genesis to Revelation. Each entry provides the context by inserting a portion of the verse along with the key word. This aids in finding the particular verse you are seeking.

Most Study Bibles include a short concordance.

Choosing a Bible concordance

There are three excellent concordances for the *King James Version/AV*: *Cruden's*, *Young's* and *Strong's*. *Young's* and *Strong's* are massive and exhaustive and ideal for very detailed Bible study.

Many modern translations of the Bible have their own concordances. It's possible that you may be able to match up your favorite Bible version with a companion Bible concordance.

Why bother with Crudens' concordance?

If you were brought up on the *KJV/Authorized Version* of the Bible you may find that many of its words and phrases are permanently lodged in your mind.

For example, you may find that you want to locate the story of the man from whom Jesus expelled many demons. All you can remember is that his name was "Legion." If you are presently now using *The Good News Bible* you won't find a reference to this story from the word "Legion."

A concordance such as *Cruden's* will guide you to Mark 5:9. Then in your *Good News Bible* you will see that the word "Mob" is used for "Legion."

simple start

Look up the word "gentle" in a concordance. You will see that the word "gentleness" follows "gentle", so it is worthwhile looking up the instances of "gentleness" as well.

This will give you a partial picture of the Bible's teaching on the subject of being gentle. There are numerous examples of gentleness in the Bible where the actual word "gentle" is not used. However, by doing this Bible study you will have a good idea about the Bible's basic teaching on this topic.

As you look up each verse ask yourself what it teaches about gentleness.

Gentle and gentleness

Old Testament instances of "gentle"
Dt 28:54; 28:56
2 Sa 18:5
1 Ki 19:12
Job 41:3
Pr 15:1; 25:15
Jer 11:19
Zec 9:9

New Testament instances of "gentle"
Mt 11:29; 21:5
Ac 27:13
1 Co 4:21
Eph 4:2
1 Th 2:7
1 Ti 3:3
1 Pe 3:4

New Testament instances of "gentleness"

2 Co 10:1	By the meekness and gentleness of Christ,
Gal 5:23	faithfulness, gentleness and self-control.
Php 4:5	Let your gentleness be evident to all.
Col 3:12	kindness, humility, gentleness and patience.
1 Ti 6:11	faith, love, endurance and gentleness.
1 Pe 3:15	But do this with gentleness and respect,

23

SOLID BIBLE STUDY

Use a Bible concordance to develop your own Bible study of the nine characteristics which make up the fruit of the Spirit.

"But the fruit of the Spirit is love, joy, peace, patience, kindness, goodness, faithfulness, gentleness and self-control." Galatians 5:22-23

Leave the research and study of "love" until the end as it will be a very long study.

Using Strong's concordance

Strong's Exhaustive Concordance
- *Strong's Exhaustive Concordance* is well named.
- It is a treasure store for any "strong" Bible student.
- It is based on the *KJV* or *Authorized Version* of the Bible.
- It lists every occurrence of every word in the Bible.

Under the word "repent"
If you look up the word "repent" you will find 45 verses in which "repent" occurs. The panel below gives five examples of

the word "repent" from these 45 verses. The numbers following the book/chapter/verse notation are explained on pages 26 and 27.

Examples of verses with "repent" in it		
the people **r** when they see war	Ex 13:17	5162
r of this evil against thy people	Ex 32:12	5162
began to preach, and to say, **R**	Mt 4:17	3340
but, except ye **r**, ye shall all	Lk 13:3	3340
be zealous therefore, and **r**	Rev 3:19	3340

Other forms of the word "repent"

Strong's Exhaustive Concordance also provides all forms in which the word "repent" occurs in the Bible. The following entries reveal six additional variations for the word "repent."

Forms of "repent"	Number of occurrences
Repentance	26
Repented	32
Repentest	1
Repenteth	5
Repenting	1
Repentings	1

The panel below gives an example from each of the above six listings.

Repentance	the righteous, but sinners to **r**	Mt 9:13	3341
Repented	for they **r** at the preaching of	Lk 11:32	3340
Repentest	kindness, and **r** thee of the evil	Jonah 4:2	5162
Repenteth	in heaven over one sinner that **r**	Lk 15:7	3340
Repenting	I am weary with **r**	Jer 15:6	5162
Repentings	my **r** are kindled together	Hos 11:8	5150

Using Strong's numbering system
Researching Greek and Hebrew words

Every occurrence of every word — plus Greek and Hebrew words

In addition to listing every occurrence of every word in the Bible, *Strong's Exhaustive Concordance* points you to the Greek and Hebrew words behind the English translation.

Strong's numbering system

The verses on pages 24-25 of the book are taken from *Strong's Exhaustive Concordance* where numbers appear after many of the words.

These numbers are the key that will lead you to the original Greek and Hebrew words. As previously noted each entry in *Strong's Exhaustive Concordance* consists of three parts. From left to right they are:

• The specific reference word along with the surrounding scripture text.
• The book, chapter and verse where the specific word is found.
• And the precise number to the Hebrew and Greek dictionaries in the back of the concordance.

The Old Testament number for repent

The number 5162, for "repent" as it occurs in the Old Testament, leads you to Strong's *Dictionary of the words in the Hebrew Bible*. Under the number 5162 you will find the following entry.

5162 נחם **nâcham**, *naw-kham'*; a prim. root; prop. to *sigh*, i.e. *breathe* strongly; by impl. *to be sorry*, i.e. (in a favorable sense) to *pity*, *console* or (reflex.) *Rue*; or (unfavorably) to 1∫ (oneself):—comfort (self), ease [one's self], repent (-er, -ing, self).

The New Testament number for repent

The number 3340, for "repent" as it occurs in the New Testament, leads you to *Strong's Dictionary of the Greek Testament*. Under the number 3340 you will find the following entry.

3340 μετανοεω **mĕtanŏĕō**, *met-an-ŏ-eh-o*; from 3326 and 3539; to *think differently* or *afterwards*, i.e. *reconsider* (mor. *feel compunction*):—repent.

You can see that the numbers in italics refer to words as they occur in the New Testament.

SOLID
BIBLE STUDY

Look up the remaining Hebrew and Greek numbers for repentance by searching in the Hebrew and Greek dictionaries.
These remaining numbers will take you to other derivative words.
• The Old Testament numbers are: **7725**; **5164**; **5150**.
• The New Testament numbers are: **3341**; **278**.

New Testament Greek
for beginners

New Testament Greek

The Greek in which the New Testament is written is not the same as classical Greek or the Greek spoken in Greece today.

New Testament Greek is known as *koinē*, or common Greek, a simple form of classical Greek. In the apostle Paul's day *koinē* Greek was spoken by all the countries surrounding the Mediterranean Sea.

From Alpha to Omega

From the above alphabet it is easy to see that the first and last letters of the Greek alphabet are A and Ω.

Jesus is given the title of being the "Alpha" and the "Omega" in the book of Revelation. Revelation 1:8; 21:6 and 22:13. "I am the Alpha and the Omega." In each case the text reads, "αλφα ... ω," with the first letter of the Greek alphabet, A, written out in full: *alpha*; and the last letter of the Greek alphabet, Ω, written out as a lower case single letter: ω.

A characteristic of God, the originator of all things, is applied to Jesus.

Transliterations

In many Bible commentaries Greek words are used. So a commentary on Romans 1:16 may point out that the Greek word for "power" is δυναμις. "I am not ashamed of the gospel, because it is the *power* of God for the salvation of everyone who believes: for the Jew, then for the Gentile,"

Often, letters from the English alphabet are used, for the benefit of non-Greek readers. So the word is printed *dunamis*.

Such transliterations often shed light on the text. In this case *dunamis* is the word from which our word dynamite is derived. So Paul is writing that the gospel has dynamite like power.

The Greek Alphabet

Even if you never study Greek you can derive a number of benefits in your Bible research if you know a little about Greek.

Greek capital letter	Greek small letter	English name of letter	English equivalent
A	α	Alpha	a
B	β	Bēta	b
Γ	γ	Gamma	g
Δ	δ	Delta	d
E	ε	Epsilon	e
Z	ζ	Zēta	z
H	η	Ēta	ē
Θ	θ	Thēta	th
I	ι	Iōta	i
K	κ	Kappa	k
Λ	λ	Lambda	i
M	μ	Mu	m
N	ν	Nu	n
Ξ	ξ	Xi	x
O	o	Omĩcron	o
Π	π	Pi	p
P	ρ	Rhō	r
Σ	σ, ς	Sigma	s
T	τ	Tau	t
Y	υ	Upsilon	u
Φ	φ	Phi	ph
X	χ	Chi	ch
Ψ	ψ	Psi	sō
Ω	ω	Ō	ō

A little more Greek

Four loves: love, love, love and love

When the writers of the New Testament wanted to convey what they meant by God's love for us, as displayed in Jesus, they had a problem. They had three Greek words for "love" but none of them expressed what they were trying to communicate. So the writers of the New Testament used a little-used term in classical Greek, *agape*. This word is transformed in the New Testament into the most powerful word imaginable for love.

1. Eros (εροσ)

The New Testament writers never use this Greek word. In classical Greek it stood for sexual love, but in the world of the Greeks and Romans it had become so badly debased that it stood for lust. So the New Testament avoids it altogether. The word "erotic" is derived from *eros*.

2. Storgē (στοργη)

This Greek word stood for the natural affection between a child and a mother. But this was not the kind of love the writers of the New Testament meant by God's great love for us and so they did not use this word either.

3. Philia (φιλια)

Philia stands for affection between friends. *Philia*, and compound words constructed from its root, like *philadelphia*, are used in the New Testament and describe warm caring relationships between people.

4. Agapē (αγαπη)

Agape is a word which hardly occurs in classical Greek, but it is the one which the writers of the New Testament used of God's special self-giving love as it was displayed in Jesus. *Agapē*-love, Godlike love, is distinguished from the other three loves.

Examples of the use of *agapē*
- John 13:35
- John 14:15
- 2 Corinthians 5:14
- 1 Thessalonians 1:3
- 1 Thessalonians 3:6
- 1 John 5:3
- 2 John 1, 3, 5, 6
- 3 John 1, 6
- Revelation 2:4

Examples of the use of *philia*
- Romans 12:10
- 1 Thessalonians 4:9
- 2 Peter 1:7

The secret sign of the fish

- In the early days of Christianity the first Christians were often persecuted. As a result they used a number of secret signs with hidden meanings.
- In the catacombs underneath the city of Rome, the Christians held secret services of worship and buried their dead friends. They sometimes scratched the sign of the fish on the walls of these underground passages.

- You may have seen the sign of the fish yourself. Some people wear a small fish badge or broach. Others have the sign of the fish on the bumpers of their cars.
- So why the fish? The Greek word for fish is ichthus. Ichthus in the Greek alphabet (ιχθυς) can become the acronym below.

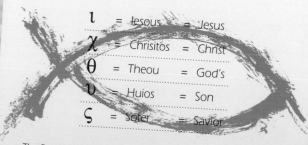

ι	= Iesous	= Jesus
χ	= Chrisitos	= Christ
θ	= Theou	= God's
υ	= Huios	= Son
ς	= soter	= Savior

The first Christians used the symbol of the fish to identify themselves as followers of Jesus Christ, God's Son and Savior.

Using a Greek-English Interlinear New Testament

Finding the exact meaning

English translations sometimes struggle to convey the exact meaning of a Greek word. As an example, it is not always easy to tell which meaning of the word "love" is being referred to in some Bible versions. The *King James Version* uses both the words "charity" and "love" to refer to *agape*. The *New International Version* uses "love" for *agape* and "brotherly love" for *philia*. The *New American Standard Bible* uses "love" in 1 Thessalonians 4:9, in which *philia* is used, and "love" in 1 Thessalonians 3:6, where *agape* is used.

How it works

A Greek-English interlinear New Testament has every Greek word of the New Testament on one line with the English word written underneath. The following verse from 1 Corinthians shows how it works.

---

1 Corinthians 13:1

Below the interlinear extract are various English translations for comparison.

Εαν	ταις γλωσςαις	των ανθῶπων	λαλω	και	των	αννγελων
If	in the tonguges	– of men	I speak	and	–	of angels

αγαπην	δε	μη	εχω...
but love			I have not

- *KJV* Though I speak with the tongues of men and of angels, and have not charity,
- *NRSV* If I speak in the tongues of mortals and of angels, but do not have love,
- *NIV* If I speak in the tongues of men and of angels, but have not love,
- *RSV* If I speak in the tongues of men and of angels, but have not love,

Comparing the KJV with the Greek

Note the use of the word "love" (loving) in the following verse from 1 Corinthians. The verb form of αγαπη (*agape*) is used and occurs as αγαπωσιν (*agaposin*).

---

1 Corinthians 2:9

αλλα καθωσ	γεγραπται		α
but as	it is has been written: Things which		

οφθαλμοσ	ουκ ειδεν	και	ουσ	ουκ	ηκουσεν
eye	saw not	and	ear		heard not

και επι	καρδιαν	ανθρωπου	ουκ	ανεβη,
and on	heart	of man		came not up,

οσα	ητοιμασεν	ο θεοσ	τοισ		αγαπωσιν
how many	prepared	– God	for the [ones]		loving

αυτον.
him.

• **KJV** "But as it is written, Eye hath not seen, nor ear heard, neither have entered into the heart of man, the things which God hath prepared for them that love him."

SOLID BIBLE STUDY

- Read 1 Corinthians 13 in an interlinear New Testament, and note the Greek word for love, agape (or one of its forms such as agapain [αγαπην]).
- Read other famous Bible verses which contain the word love in this way. Observe which Greek word is used for love.
- Read John 3:16, John 15:13, Romans 8:39, 1 Thessalonians 3:6, 1 Thessalonians 4:9, 1 John 4:7-8

Using an expository dictionary of Bible words

Vine's Expository Dictionary of New Testament Words

Using an expository Bible dictionary, such as Vine's *Expository Dictionary of New Testament Words*, gives you both a definition and a summary of the Bible's teaching on hundreds of the most important Bible words. Look at the following entry on "reconcile". Note that *Vine's Dictionary* provides other derivates under the heading of Reconcile, Reconciliation.

Look up other important linked words to reconcile in an expository word dictionary of the Bible. Try the following words: "reconciliation, peace, unity."

RECONCILE, RECONCILIATION

A. Verbs.

1. *katallassō* (καταλλάσσω, 2644) properly denotes "to change, exchange" (especially of money); hence, of persons, "to change from enmity to friendship, to reconcile." With regard to the relationship between God and man, the use of this and connected words shows that primarily "reconciliation" is what God accomplishes, exercising His grace towards sinful man on the ground of the death of Christ in propitiatory sacrifice under the judgment due to sin, 2 Cor. 5:19, where both the verb and the noun are used. By reason of this men in their sinful condition and alienation from God are invited to be "reconciled" to Him; that is to say, to change their attitude, and accept the provision God had made, whereby their sins can be remitted and they themselves be justified in His sight in Christ.

Rom. 5:10 expresses this in another way: "For if, while we were enemies, we were reconciled to God through the death of His Son...;" that we were "enemies" not only expresses man's hostile attitude to God but signifies that until this change of attitude takes place men are under condemnation, exposed to God's wrath. The death of His Son is the means of the removal of this, and thus we "receive the reconciliation," Rom. 5:11, RV. This stresses the attitude of God's favor toward us ...

2. *apokatallassō* (ἀποκατάλλασσω, 604) "to reconcile completely", "to change from one condition to another," so as to remove all enmity and leave no

impediment to unity and peace used in Eph. 2:16, of the "reconciliation" of believing Jew and Gentile "in one body unto God through the Cross;" in Col. 1:21 not the union of Jew and Gentile is in view, but the change wrought in the individual believer from alienation and enmity, on account of evil works, to "reconciliation" with God; in Col. 1:20 the word is used of the Divine purpose to "reconcile" through Christ "all things unto Himself ... whether things upon the earth, or things in the heavens," the basis of the change being the peace effected "through the blood of His Cross."

3. *diallassō* (διαλλάσσω, 1259) "to effect an alteration, exchange," and hence, "to reconcile," in cases of mutual hostility yielding to mutual concession, is used in the Passive Voice in Matt. 5:24, which illustrates the point. There is no such idea as "making it up" where God and man are concerned.

B. Noun.

katallagē (καταλλαγή, 2643) akin to A, No 1, primarily "an exchange," denotes "reconciliation," a change on the part of one party, induced by an action on the part of another; in the NT, the "reconciliation" of men to God by His grace and love in Christ. The word is used in Rom. 5:11; 11:15. The word also occurs in 2 Cor. 5:18,19, where "the ministry of reconciliation" and "the word of reconciliation" are not the ministry of teaching the doctrine of expiation, but that of beseeching men to be "reconciled" to God on the ground of what God has wrought in

35

Using a Bible dictionary

A Bible dictionary

A Bible dictionary provides definitive and descriptive information on Bible words. It may even include devotional material about Bible topics which is not always found in expository dictionaries of Bible words.

The following extract below is from *Easton's Bible Dictionary*.

REPENTANCE

There are three Greek words used in the New Testament to denote repentance.

1. The verb metamelomai is used of a change of mind, such as to produce regret or even remorse on account of sin, but not necessarily a change of heart. This word is used with reference to the repentance of Judas (Matt. 27:3).

2. Metanoeo, meaning to change one's mind and purpose, as the result of after knowledge. This verb, with (3.) the cognate noun metanoia, is used of true repentance, a change of mind and purpose and life, to which remission of sin is promised.

Evangelical repentance

Evangelical repentance consists of:
1. a true sense of one's own guilt and sinfulness;
2. an apprehension of God's mercy in Christ;
3. an actual hatred of sin (Ps. 119:128; Job 42:5, 6; 2 Cor. 7:10) and turning from it to God; and
4. a persistent endeavour after a holy life in a walking with God in the way of his commandments.

The true penitent

The true penitent is conscious:
• of guilt (Ps. 51:4, 9),
• of pollution (Ps. 51:5, 7, 10),
• and of helplessness (Ps. 51:11; 109:21, 22).

Thus he apprehends himself to be just what God has always seen him to be and declares him to be. But repentance comprehends not only such a sense of sin, but also an apprehension of mercy, without which th_____ ___ __ o true rep____ tan___

Using a topical Bible

What are topical keywords?

Nave's Topical Bible is a comprehensive digest of over 20,000 topics and sub-topics with more than 1,000,000 Scripture references. It groups verses by "ideas" or "topics", thus offering a better overview of relevant Scriptures than a concordance. It provides a cross-reference system and includes the full text of the verse cited in most instances.

Nave's Topical Bible

By using *Nave's Topical Bible* many fruitful avenues for extended Bible Study are opened up, as is seen from the following entry on "repentance".

Repentance

Instances of: Joseph's brethren, of their maltreatment of Joseph, Gen. 42:21; 50:17,18. Pharaoh, of his hardness of heart, Ex. 9:27; 10:16,17. Balaam, of his spiritual blindness, Num. 22:34, with vs. 24-35. Israelites, of worshiping the golden calf, Ex 33:3,4; of their murmuring on account of lack of bread and water, when the plague of fiery serpents came upon them, Num. 21:4-7; when rebuked by an angel for not expelling the Canaanites, Judg. 2:1-5; of their idolatry, when afflicted by the Philistines, Judg. 10:6-16; 1 Sam. 7:3-6; in asking for a king, 1 Sam. 12:16-20; in the time of Asa, under the preaching of Azariah, 2 Chr. 15:1-19; under the preaching of Obed, 2 Chr. 28:9-11; under the influence of Hezekiah, 2 Chr. 30:11. Achan, of his theft, Josh. 7:20. Saul, at the reproof of Samuel for not destroying the Amaletkites, 1 Sam. 15:24, with vs. 6-31. David, at the rebuke of Nathan, the prophet, of his sins of adultery and murder, 2 ... 12:11,13, with vs. 7 ... PSALMS, PENE...

Exemplified: Num. 21:7. Therefo... the people came to Moses, and sai... We have sinned, for we have spoken against the Lord, and against thee: pray unto the Lord, that he take aw... the serpents form us. And Moses prayed for the people.

2 Sam. 24:10. David's heart smo... him after that he had numbered th... people. And David said unto the Lord, I have sinned greatly in that I have done: and now, I beseech thee, O Lord, take away the iniquity of thy servant; for I have done very fooli... ly. 17. And David spake unto t... Lord when he saw the angel tha... smote the people, and said, Lo, I have sinned, and I have done wickedly: but these sheep, what have they done? let thine hand, I pray thee, b... against me, and against my father ... house. 1 Chr. 21:17.

2 Chr. 29:6. Our fathers have tres... passed, and done that which was evil in the eyes of the Lo... have forsaken hi... away their ...

Using a one volume Bible commentary

One volume commentaries

The best type of commentary to use or buy initially is a one volume commentary. Although they are often large in size they do offer you comments on some of the most significant and difficult passages in the Bible. Plus, they provide an introduction, background information and commentary notes on each book of the Bible. An excellent, devotional, one-volume classic commentary is by Matthew Henry. A simpler one-volume commentary is the *Concise Bible Commentary* by James Gray.

Psalm 51

Psalm 51 records David's heartfelt repentance. The following extract is taken from the commentary on Psalm 51 by John W. Baigent, found in *The International Bible Commentary*, (General Editor, F.F. Bruce) which is based on the NIV.

A PRAYER FOR FORGIVENESS

This individual lament is most suitably called a "Penitential Psalm". The heading links it with the experience of David recorded in 2 Samuel 11-12, and it obviously fits that situation, ... being an expansion of David's confession of 2 Samuel 12:13.

The psalm opens (vv. 1,2) with the urgent plea for forgiveness, based upon the psalmist's knowledge of the merciful character of God (cf. Exod. 34:6f.). The genuineness of his confession is demonstrated by his profound understanding of the true nature of sin in its outward, inward and Godward aspects (vv. 3-5). Verses 6-12 express his deep desire for inward cleansing and spiritual renewal; whilst vv. 13-17 declare his determination to show his gratitude not only in humble thanksgiving, but also in a public testimony to the saving acts of God (cf Psalms 9:1f.; 22; 25; 40:9f.). The conclusion (vv. 18,19) asks that God will enable Jerusalem to be rebuilt so that the c̶lic observances, impossible to c̶ out during the exile, may be ̶ned, to the pleasure of God.

̶ on or "be gracious ̶ally expresses

inferior, carrying with it the idea of unmerited favor. **your great compassion**: lit. "The multitude of thy mercies"; "mercies" here represents a word which in the singular usually means "womb" (cf. Isa. 49:15) or "Bowels" (cf. Phil. 2:1, AV), thus it signifies deeply-felt compassion. **blot out**: as from a book (cf. Exod. 32:32; Neh. 13:14). **wash**: the verb is used of washing clothes by treading them (cf. Exod. 19:10, 14; 2 Sam. 19:24; Jer. 2:22). **3. I know**: or "I acknowledge" RV (cf. Isa. 49:12). **4**. Sin, even when directed against one's fellow man, is in the last analysis rebellion against God: "sin is ultimately a religious concept rather than an ethical one" (Weiser). Cf. 2 Sam. 12:13; Gen. 39:9; Prov. 14:13; 17:5. so that: his confession of culpability reveals the justice of God's punishment (cf. Jos. 7:19). **justified**: lit. "Clear". 5. There is no suggestion here that the processes of birth or conception are sinful in themselves, nor that the birth of the psalmist was illegitimate. "The Psalmist confesses his total involvement in human sinfulness, from the very beginning of his existence" (A.A. Anderson). This is not offered as an excuse, but rather as an additional evidence ̶ his ut̶ ̶ulness (c̶ 58:3).

Using a commentary on a specific book of the Bible

Building up a library

It's possible to build one's own personal library with a variety of excellent Bible commentaries. Many helpful sets of Bible commentaries on each book of the Bible exist.

A book devoted to a single book of the Bible gives a much more detailed commentary than a one-volume commentary. The following extract is taken from *The Message of Acts*, by John Stott. It is commentary on part of the first recorded Christian sermon after the death of Jesus, in which Peter stresses the importance of repentance.

Acts 2:38–39

³⁸Peter replied, "Repent and be baptized, every one of you, in the name of Jesus Christ for the forgiveness of your sins. And you will receive the gift of the Holy Spirit. ³⁹The promise is for you and your children and for all who are far off — for all whom the Lord our God will call."

Cut to the heart, that is, convicted of sin and conscience-stricken, Peter's hearers asked anxiously what they should do (37). Peter replied that they must *repent*, completely changing their mind about Jesus and their attitude to him, and *be baptized* in his name, submitting to the humiliation of baptism, which Jews regarded as necessary for Gentile converts only, and submitting to it in the name of the very person they had obviously rejected. This would be a clear, public token of their repentance — and of their faith in him. Though Peter does not specifically call on the crowd to believe, they evidently did so, since they are termed "believers" in verse 44, and in any case repentance and faith involve each other, the turn from sin being impossible without the turn to God, and vice versa (cf. 3:19). And both are signified by baptism in Christ's name, which means "by his authority, acknowledging his claims, subscribing to his doctrines, engaging in his service, and relying on his merits" (I. Alexander).

Then they would receive two free gifts of God — the forgiveness of their sins (even of the sin of rejecting God's Christ) and the gift of the Holy Spirit (to regenerate, indwell, unite and transform them). For they must not imagine that the Pentecostal gift was for the apostles alone, or for the 120 disciples who had waited ten days for the Spirit to come, for any élitist group, or even for that nation or that generation alone. God had placed no such limitations on his offer and gift. On the contrary (39), *the promise* — or "gift" or "baptism" — of the Spirit (1:4; 2:33) was for them also (who were listening to Peter), and for all who were far off (certainly the Jews of the dispersion and perhaps also prophetically the distant Gentile world, as in Is. 49:1, 12; 57:19; cf. Eph. 2:13, 17), indeed *for all* (without exception) *whom the Lord our God will call.* Everyone God calls to himself through Christ receives both gifts. The gifts of God are coextensive with the call of God.

Using a Bible handbook

Bible handbooks and Bible encyclopedia

It is often difficult to draw distinctions between books which are published under the names of Bible handbooks and encyclopedia. They often cover the same ground and the good ones are invaluable as reference tools for Bible study. A Bible handbook provides additional, interesting information often not found in other research tools.

The following two extracts are taken from *The New Unger's Bible Handbook* (revised by Gary N. Larson) and shed light on the subject of repentance with special reference to the Old Testament sacrificial system and to redemption in the New Testament.

A theological explanation of the Old Testament sacrificial system

The sacrificial system When Moses led Israel out of Egypt, the sacrificial system was given fresh meaning in the light of experienced redemption, organized, codified and written down by inspiration in the sacrificial codes of Exodus and Leviticus.

Meaning of sacrifices for the Old Testament worshiper The fundamental idea to the Hebrew worshiper of the sacrifices was that they were a *means of approach to God*. This is evident from the underlying connotation of the broadest Hebrew term for "sacrifice" (*qorban* from the root *qrb*, "to draw near or approach"). Sinful, guilty man needed some way to draw near to the infinitely holy God with assurance of acceptance. This was divin...

The application of the Old Testament sacrifices

The typological meaning of the sacrifices For the New Testament believer the Old Testament sacrificial system is particularly instructive through its illustrations of New Testament redemption. Many of the Levitical prescriptions are typical, i.e., they were symbolically *predictive*, expressing a need that they could not satisfy, but which the coming promised Redeemer would fulfill (Eph 5:2; 1 Cor 10:11, Heb 9:14). Others serve as principles that can be applied to the New Testament dispensation, while yet others illustrate facets of God's interaction with man that are timeless in their application. This is the normal application of the Old Testament sacrifices for the New Testament believer, although not their basic or practi...al meaning for the Old ...ment

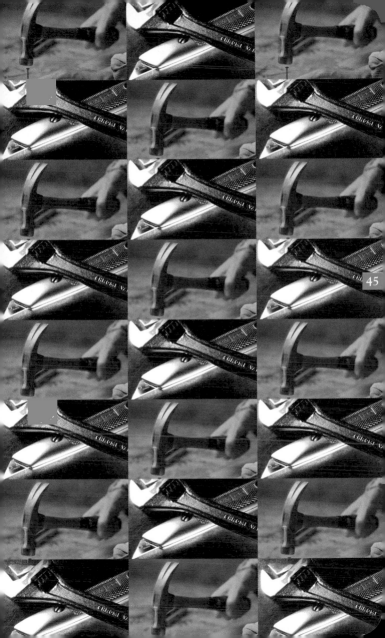

Using a Bible atlas

Key maps

Bible atlases are probably one of the most underused and
undervalued of all the Bible reference tools. In order to
appreciate the insight that you can gain from using maps,
examine these map topics in a good Study Bible:

- The physical map of
  Palestine
- The ancient world at the
  time of the patriarchs
- The Exodus
- The empire of David and
  Solomon
- The kingdoms of Israel and
  Judah
- Palestine in New Testament
  times

- Jesus' Galilean ministry
- Jesus' later ministry
- Jerusalem at the time of
  Jesus
- Journeys of the apostles
- Paul's first journey
- Paul's second journey
- Paul's third journey
- Paul's journey to Rome

SOLID
BIBLE STUDY

1. Follow Paul's third
missionary journey, Acts
18:23–21:16 and his journey
to Rome, Acts 21:26–28:29, in
the Acts of the Apostles with
the help of good maps.
2. Locate on a map the
destination of Paul's letters and
see how many of them you
can tie in to his pioneer
missionary tours recorded in
the Acts of the Apostles. For
example Acts 16:1 recounts
where Paul met Timothy, who
became his protégé, and to
whom he wrote 1 and 2
Timothy.

Reading the Acts of the Apostles with maps

The dramatic spread of the Christian gospel after Jesus' ascension is described in the Acts of the Apostles. It is impossible to fully appreciate what is recorded in the Acts of the Apostles without referring to maps.

"But you will receive power when the Holy Spirit comes on you, and you will be my witnesses in Jerusalem, and in all Judea and Samaria, and to the ends of the earth." *Acts 1:8*

Paul's first missionary journey
Acts 13:2–14:8
Turn to a map of Paul's first missionary journey and look up the following places as you read Acts 13:2–14:8 and see what happened in each place.

Bible reference	Map location
13:3	Seleucia
13:4	Salamis
13:4	Cyprus
13:6	Paphos
13:13	Perga
13:14-50	Pisidian Antioch
13:51–14:5	Iconium
14:6-19	Lystra
14:20-21	Derbe "They preached the good news in that city [Derbe] and won a large number of disciples." *Acts 14:21*
14:21	Lystra, Iconium and Antioch (revisited)
14:24	Pamphylia
14:25	Perga
14:25	Attalia
14:26	Antioch

Paul's second missionary journey
Acts 15:36–18:22
"Paul said to Barnabas, 'Let us go back and visit the brothers in all the towns where we preached the word of the Lord and see how they are doing.'" *Acts 1:36*

Bible reference	Map location
16:1-4	Derbe, Lystra, Iconium, Antioch
16:8	Troas
16:11	Samothrace and Neapolis
16:12-40	Philippi
17:1-10	Thessalonica
17:10-14	Berea
17:15-34	Athens
18:1-18	Corinth
18:18	Cenchrea
18:19-21	Ephesus
18:22	Caesarea, Antioch

Using a Bible theology book

The value of a Bible theology book

Good Bible theology books normally give the following information on Bible topics:

- A comparison between Old Testament teaching and New Testament teaching
- The meaning of the Hebrew or Greek word
- Links with other important Bible topics
- An aspect about the topic which must not be missed
- Mistakes about the topic that have been made
- Confusions to avoid

The following extract, written by R. Kearsley, is taken from *The New Dictionary of Theology* (edited by S.B. Ferguson and D.F. Wright).

REPENTANCE.

The OT often speaks of repentance to describe Israel's turning back to their God (e.g. 2 Ch. 7:17), in response to a promise of restored fortunes for the nation. In the NT, however, the preaching of repentance is greatly heightened and given specific content for the individual. This feature starts with the preaching of John the Baptist (Mt. 3:5-12; Lu. 3:7-14). The Gk. words used throughout the NT are mainly forms related to the verb *metanoein*, "to change one's mind". This small phrase, however, describes a radical change in the individual's *disposition*, for the change of mind concerns his judgment upon himself and his sin together with an evaluation of God's demands upon him. The transformation implied, therefore, is not a matter merely of mental judgment, but of new religious and moral attitudes (a turning to *God*, 1 Thes. 1:9) and a new behavior (Acts 26:20), as John's preaching spelt out.

A continuous process

The importance of repentance is seen from the early preaching of the apostles and from its place as the first principle of the Christian message (Heb 6:1). Although there is in conversion a decisive change of mind, the renewing of the mind towards God is a *continuous* process (Rom 12:2; Eph. 4:23) just as faith is to be increased. Turning, and renewal of faith in the Christian's life, are the active side of the process called sanctification, of which regeneration and preservation are the passive aspects.

Martin Luther

Due to the increased emphasis on penitence (sorrow for sin) associated with repentance, the idea of confession and penance came to overshadow the sense of "changing one's mind", and it was Martin Luther who rediscovered the NT Gk. word, *metanoein*. With this he replaced the prevailing Latin Vulgate rendering of "do penance", and allied repentance closely to faith.

A moral act

It cannot be stressed too much that repentance is a moral act involving the turning of the whole person in spirit, mind and will to consent, and subjection, to the will of God. It is in a very real sense a moral miracle, a gift of grace. Terms often confused with repentance, such as pe̶̶̶̶ remorse or penance, do n̶̶̶ tice to the impact of ̶̶̶ call repentance.

Using Bible computer software

Computer software

Computer software offers many benefits for Bible study. More and more Bible research tools are becoming available for computer. Most are obtaianble in CD-ROM format. Often times a CD-ROM is less expensive than the book. The one described on these two pages relates to the *New Living Translation*, the successor of the *Living Bible*.

If you are connected to the Internet, many resources are available for your use and are free of charge. See the pull-out chart in the back for a wonderful Bible research resource.

Quickverse Life Application Bible

Topic index	The Bible text

1. Touch points

This allows you to see short summaries of dozens of topics. Under "repentance" you will find:

■ Why is repentance necessary?
■ What is repentance?
■ Is repentance a one-time event, or do we need to repent each time we sin?

Each question is answered with relevant Bible verses and a short explanation.

2. Bible topics

This is a fuller article about the Bible's teaching on repentance. It has hundreds of verses to look up, as well as numerous headings, such as:

■ Repentance attributed to God
■ Exhortation to repentance
■ Examples of repentance
■ Bible passages which exemplify repentance

In the Bible text there is often a symbol to press which gives you the Greek text for a particular word or phrase.

At Mark 1:4, for example reads in the *NLT*, "preaching that people should be baptized to show that they had turned from their sins and turned to God to be forgiven."

On pressing the symbol after the word "forgiven" the following message appears on your screen: "Mark 1:4 Greek: [this is an invitation for the viewer to look up this verse in a Greek New Testament to see the significance of some Greek word used.] 'preaching a baptism of repentance for the forgiveness of sins.'"

Insights

The Bible text has another symbol in it which takes you to insights on particular verses.

For example, the insight symbol at Matthew 4:17 takes you to an explanation about repentance. This says that repentance is turning away from self-centeredness and turning our live over to Christ's control.

Multi-media index

This gives a selection of maps, art, photographs, photo-bubbles, dramatic readings and time-lines.

One of the photographs is entitled "Pergamum overview" and is a dramatic shot of the ruins of Pergamum. This church was told to "repent" in Revelation 2:16.

Search facility

By typing in the word "repent" 157 related articles in various programs are listed.

Under the heading of "People and Places" there are 11 matching articles. One of these are the letters to the seven churches, in Revelation chapters 2-3, where you can note that five out of the seven churches are told that the action they need to take is to repent.

Good Bible software to consider:
- PC Study Bible (Bible Soft)
- Wordsearch (NavPress software)
- Nelson's Electronic Bible Reference Library (Nelson)
- QuickVerse (Parson's)
- Complete Word Study Bible (AmG Publ.)

How Jesus used Scripture

Our view of Scripture will determine how much we study it

Perhaps the most important reason for studying Scripture is not our own evaluation of it, but Jesus' evaluation. Because we believe that Jesus is the Son of God, we seek to follow his teaching on this subject and his submissive, humble attitude towards Scripture.

"The scripture cannot be broken." *John 10:35*

1. Jesus' behavior was in line with the Old Testament

When Jesus was tempted by Satan, (Matthew 4:1-11), he quoted Scripture in the presence of the devil. What the Scripture said – Jesus did.

When the devil offered Jesus the kingdoms of this world, Jesus replied, "Away from me, Satan! For it is written: 'Worship the Lord your God, and serve him only.'" *Matthew 4:10*

Jesus is quoting from Deuteronomy 6:13. Jesus also quotes Deuteronomy 8:3 and 6:16 in this incident.

Gegraptai … gegraptai … gegraptai

In Matthew chapter 4, Jesus uses the same phrase three times in verses 4, 6 and 10: "It is written," or "It stands written." In the Greek this is the single word *gegraptai*. Whatever Scripture said settled the matter for Jesus.

2. Jesus' mission fulfilled Old Testament prophecy

Jesus knew of his role as Messiah from direct revelation, but he also could have learned of this role from the Old Testament Scripture.

- He knew that he was to be Isaiah's suffering servant, see Isaiah 52:13 53:12.
- He knew that he would fulfil the role of Daniel's son of man, see Daniel 7:13.
- This accounts for the sense of compulsion which pervaded Jesus' mission.

"He [Jesus] began to teach them that the Son of Man must

suffer many things and be rejected by the elders, chief priests and teachers of the law, and that he must be killed and after three days rise again." *Mark 8:31*

3. Jesus submitted to the Old Testament's teaching in matters of controversy

When in dispute with the religious leaders of his day Jesus went to the Scriptures as his only court of appeal.

When asked a question to test him, by a teacher of the law, Jesus asked, "What is written in the Law?" and, "How do you read it?" *Luke 10:26*

When the chief priests, the teachers of the law and the elders tried to trip Jesus up with their questions and arguments, Jesus asked them, "Haven't you read this scripture ...?" *Mark 12:10*

Jesus roundly condemned the practice of adding to the Scriptures which the Pharisees were so guilty of. "You have let go of the commands of God and are holding on to the traditions of men. ... You have a fine way of setting aside the commands of God in order to observe your own traditions! ... Thus you nullify the word of God by your tradition that you have handed down." *Mark 7:8-9, 13*

Cruden's prayer

When Alexander Cruden finished his concordance of the King James Version of the Bible in 1737 he wrote the following prayer in the preface to its first edition:

I conclude this preface with praying that God, who has graciously enabled me to bring this large work to a conclusion, would make it useful to those who seriously and carefully search the Scriptures; and grant that the sacred writings, which are so important and worthy of high esteem, may meet with all that affection and regard which they deserve. May those who profess to believe the Scriptures to be a revelation from God, apply themselves to the reading and study of them; and may they, by the Holy Spirit of God, who inspired the Scriptures, be made wise for salvation through faith which is in Christ Jesus, Amen.

Finding the Old Testament in the New Testament

Watch closely for Old Testament references

In the Gospels there are about 100 different references to the Old Testament.

The letter to the Hebrews, alone, also has about 100 references to the Old Testament.

If you read a New Testament verse and don't realize that a specific quote or teaching is from the Old Testament, you may miss the complete meaning of the verse.

"I am the true vine"

It is not necessary to know the Old Testament background to John 15:1-8 in order to understand what Jesus means when he says in verse one: "I am the true vine."

But your appreciation is enhanced when you realize that Jesus' hearers would have immediately linked up such a thought with Psalm 80:8-11 and Isaiah 5:1-7. "I will sing for the one I love a song about his vineyard ..." *Isaiah 5:1*

"A landowner ... planted a vineyard"

When Jesus spoke about a vineyard in Matthew 21:33-46, his opponents were quick to see that Jesus was speaking against them, because they had such a clear appreciation of the Old Testament. "When the chief priests and the Pharisees heard Jesus' parables, they knew he was talking about them. They looked for a way to arrest him." *Matthew 21:45-46*

The book of Revelation

The book of Revelation has almost three hundred quotations from or allusions to the Old Testament. The more you are aware of them the more you will appreciate the message of Revelation.

Topic	Ref(s)	Old Testament background
1. Seven spirits	1:4	Isaiah 11:2
2. The pierced Jesus	1:7	Zechariah 12:10
3. The Almighty [Christ]	1:8	Isaiah 9:6
4. Lampstands	1:12, 20	Zechariah 4:2
5. Description of Jesus	1:14-15	Daniel 7:9
6. Falling in God's presence	1:17	Ezekiel 1:28; Daniel 8:17-18
7. Tree of life	2:7	Genesis 2:9
8. The First and the Last	2:8	Isaiah 44:6
9. Teaching of Balaam	2:14	Numbers 24:12-14; 25:1-2
10. Searches hearts	2:23	Proverbs 21:2; Jeremiah 17:10
11. Broken pottery	2:27	Isaiah 30:14; Jeremiah 19:11
12. Key of David	3:7	Isaiah 22:22
13. A throne in heaven	4:2-3	Ezekiel 1:26-28
14. Four living creatures	4:6	Ezekiel 1:5
15. Root of David	5:5	Isaiah 11:1, 10
16. Colored horses	6:2-8	Zechariah 1:8-17; 6:1-8
17. Seal on foreheads	7:3	Ezekiel 9:4
18. Tear wiped away	7:17; 21:4	Isaiah 25:8
19. Hand raised to heaven	10:5	Daniel 12:7
20. Eating a scroll	10:9	Ezekiel 3:1-3
21. Dragon	13:1	Daniel 7:1-6
22. Fallen Babylon	14:8	Isaiah 21:9; Jeremiah 51:8
23. Wine of God's fury	14:10	Isaiah 51:17; Jeremiah 25:15
24. Son of man	14:14	Daniel 7:13
25. Judgment books opened	20:12	Daniel 7:9-10
26. New heaven, new earth	21:1	Isaiah 65:17
27. Glory of God's light	21:23; 22:5	Isaiah 60:19-20

Studying a long Old Testament book
An example using Isaiah

A bird's eye view
Before you think of looking at the book in any detail go for a
bird's eye view of the whole book. Skim through the book and
note how it divides up in the following sections.
- Prophecies for Judah and Jerusalem 1:1–12:6
- Prophecies about foreign nations 13:1–27:13
- Jerusalem under Assyrian rule 28:1–39:8
- The return of the exiles 40:1–66:24

At least this will tell you that the book is
full of prophecies and that Jerusalem is
a focal point.

Use keys to unlock the meaning of a book

A key verse	**Isaiah 9:6-7** It's a good idea to read such key verses and see why you think they are thought to be important.
A key word	**Salvation** Do a quick study on salvation in Isaiah and look up the following verses. Isaiah 12:2, 3; 25:9; 26:1, 18; 30:15; 33:2, 6; 45:8, 17; 46:13; 49:6, 8; 51:5, 6, 8; 52:7, 10; 56:1; 59:16, 17; 60:18; 61:10; 62:1; 63:5.
A key chapter	**Isaiah 52:13–53:12** Compare Isaiah 52:13–53:12 with Psalm 22. Other key chapters about Isaiah's ministry and message 1, 6, 9, 13, 32, 40, 44, 53, 57, 65, 66.
The author	Isaiah has been called the "St Paul of the Old Testament" and his book is often rated as among the greatest of the prophetic writings in the Bible. He started his ministry "in the year that King Uzziah died" Isaiah 6:1, 740 BC. There is a Jewish tradition that he was martyred by being sawn in two. See Hebrews 11:37.

Isaiah's characteristic name for God

Isaiah refers to God as "the Holy One of Israel." It's worth using a concordance to look up this name in Isaiah. It occurs 12 times in Isaiah chapters 1–39, and 14 times in chapters 40–66. The fact that this name for God is used only in six other places through the rest of the Old Testament supports the argument for the unity of and single authorship of the book of Isaiah.

Isaiah's distinctive methods of writing

Isaiah loved using personification.

Who/what is personified	Reference
The moon and the sun will be ashamed.	Isaiah 24:23
Desert and parched land rejoice	Isaiah 35:1
Trees clap, their hands	Isaiah 55:12
Israel is a vineyard	Isaiah 5:7
The winepress is trodden (God's judgment)	Isaiah 51:17
"Rock" is a name given to God	Isaiah 17:10

Isaiah the poet

Isaiah uses 2,200 different Hebrew words in his prophecy: more than any other Old Testament writer, and his rich poetry beautifully conveys his divine message. Read some of Isaiah's poems and hymns of praise.

- A wisdom poem *Isaiah 28:23-29*
- The vineyard song *Isaiah 5:1-7*
- Hymns of praise *Isaiah 12:1-6; 38:10-20*

Key words, key themes and key verses

A list of key verses, key themes and key verses for each book of the Bible are found in a companion book – *The Bible made easy* on pages 8-9, 12-13, 32-33.

Studying the contents of a long Old Testament book

An example using Isaiah

At some stage you must read through the book
It is much more important to expose yourself to God's Word than to read what other people have written about the Bible. Look at the main headings in the contents outline below to get your bearings. Read through Isaiah using the contents outline as your guide.

PART 1 THE BOOK OF JUDGMENT 1–39

1. **Prophecies against Judah 1–12**
   - The judgment of Judah 1:1-31
   - The day of judgment 2:1–4:6
   - The parable of the vineyard 5:1-30
   - Isaiah's commission 6:1-13
   - The destruction of Israel by Assyria 7:1–10:4
   - The destruction of Assyria by God 10:5–12:6

2. **Prophecies against other nations 13–23**
   - Prophecies against Assyria and its ruler 13:1–14:27
   - Prophecies against ten more nations: Philistia, 14:24-27; Moab, 15:1–16:14; Aram and Israel, 17:1-14; Ethiopia, 18:1-7; Egypt, 19:1–20:6; Babylon, 21:1-10; Dumah (Edom), 21:11-12; Arabia, 21:13-17; Jerusalem, 22:1-25; Tyre, 23:1-18

3. **God's word to the world 24–27**
   - Worldwide judgment 24:1-23
   - The triumphs of God's kingdom 25:1–27:13

4. **Woes and blessings 28–35**
   - Five woes on the unfaithful in Israel 28:1–32:20
   - Woe against Assyria 33:1-24
   - Woe to the nations 34:1-17
   - Blessings promised for restored Zion 35:1-10

PART 2 THE BOOK OF COMFORT 40-66

Studying the links to Jesus in a long Old Testament book

An example using Isaiah

Jesus in the prophets

"Read all the prophetic books without seeing Christ in them, and you will find nothing so insipid and flat. See Christ there, and what you read becomes fragrant."

John Chrysostom, 347-407, bishop of Constantinople

Jesus in Isaiah

Isaiah's prophecies about Jesus being the Messiah are more numerous and more specific than any other Old Testament prophet.

	Prophecy about Jesus		Prophecy fulfilled in the New Testament
1.	Isaiah 7:14	The sign of the virgin	Matthew 1:22-23
2.	Isaiah 9:1-2	Zebulun and Naphtali	Matthew 4:12-16
3.	Isaiah 9:6	A child is born	Luke 2:11
4.	Isaiah 9:6	Prince of Peace	Ephesians 2:14-18
5.	Isaiah 11:1	The stump of Jesse	Luke 3:23
6.	Isaiah 11:2	The Spirit of the Lord	Matthew 3:16
7.	Isaiah 28:16	A precious cornerstone	1 Peter 2:4-6
8.	Isaiah 40:3-5	A voice in the desert	Matthew 3:1-3
9.	Isaiah 42:1-4	A smoldering wick	Matthew 12:15-21
10.	Isaiah 42:6	A light for the Gentiles	Luke 2:29-32
11.	Isaiah 50:6	Mocking and spitting	Matthew 26:67-68
12.	Isaiah 61:1-2	The Spirit of the Lord	Luke 4:16-21

"To proclaim the year of the Lord's favor"

Jesus used words from Isaiah 61:1-2 at the beginning of his ministry to explain what he had been called to do.

> "The Spirit of the Lord is on me,
> because he has anointed me
> to preach good news to the poor.
> He has sent me to proclaim freedom for the prisoners
>   and recovery of sight to the blind,
> to release the oppressed,
>   to proclaim the year of the Lord's favor."
> *Luke 4:17-21*

The "servant songs"

The "servant songs" found in Isaiah are vivid pictures of the coming "servant of the Lord," who can be identified with the promised Messiah.

The "servant songs" of Isaiah

- Isaiah 42:1-4
- Isaiah 45:5-7
- Isaiah 49:1-6
- Isaiah 50:4-11
- Isaiah 52:13–53:12

SOLID
BIBLE STUDY

Make a devotional study of Isaiah 52:13–53:12. Note the numerous references to the death of Jesus. A Study Bible with good cross references will assist in this.

Another approach is to read the following New Testament passages, and see how each one links up with Isaiah 52:13 – 53:12: Philippians 2:7-11; Luke 23:18; John 1:11; John 7:5; Romans 5:6, 8; Matthew 27:12-14; John 1:29; 1 Peter 1:18-19; Matthew 27:57-60; Mark 15:28.

The necessity of the Holy Spirit in studying Scripture

Two essential truths
Christians believe that the Holy Spirit communicates God's truth in two ways:
- by revelation - to the writer
- by illumination - to the reader

The Bible is "God-breathed" *2 Timothy 3:16*, through the Spirit of God, and so the Bible is referredto as God's revelation to human kind.

All Christians stand in need of illumination from the same Holy Spirit as one reads and studies the Scriptures.

What kind of people does the Holy Spirit enlighten?
- Regenerate people   John 3:3
- Humble people   Matthew 11:25-26
- Obedient people   John 7:17; 14:21
- Witnessing people   Mark 4:21-24

The Holy Spirit in the New Testament
The Holy Spirit has a much more prominent role in the New Testament than in the Old Testament. In the Old Testament the Holy Spirit only came to a few people, whereas in the New Testament after the death of Jesus, he came to all men and women who believe in Jesus. See Acts 2:17.

The Spirit is called "holy" only twice in the Old Testament, (Psalm 51:11 and Isaiah 63:10), but more than 90 times in the New Testament.

SOLID
BIBLE STUDY

Use a Bible concordance to study all the times the Spirit or Holy Spirit is mentioned in the Old and New Testaments.

The centrality of the Holy Spirit in Paul's prayers

"I keep asking that the God of our Lord Jesus Christ, the glorious Father, may give you the Spirit of wisdom and revelation, so that you may know him better. I pray that

Make a study of the work of the Holy Spirit in the life of a Christian from Romans 7; 2 Corinthians 3 and Galatians 5.

the eyes of your heart may be enlightened in order that you may know the hope to which he has called you, the riches of his glorious inheritance in the saints, and his incomparably great power for us who believe." *Ephesians 1:17-19*

Also read Ephesians 3:14-19 and Colossians 1:9-14

Titles and names of the Holy Spirit in the Old Testament

Note the variety of names the Holy Spirit is given in the Old Testament. Always ask that you may be illuminated by the Holy Spirit as you study Scripture.

Bible reference	Name or title given to the Holy Spirit
Genesis 1:2	The Spirit of God
2 Chronicles 20:14	The Spirit of the Lord
Job 32:8	The breath of the Almighty
Psalm 51:11	Holy Spirit
Psalm 143:10	[God's] good Spirit
Isaiah 11:2	The Spirit of wisdom
Isaiah 11:2	The Spirit of understanding
Isaiah 11:2	The Spirit of counsel
Isaiah 11:2	The Spirit of power
Isaiah 11:2	The Spirit of knowledge
Isaiah 11:2	The Spirit of the fear of the Lord
Isaiah 61:1	The Spirit of the Sovereign Lord
Isaiah 63:10	His Holy Spirit

The Bible on Bible study

What is the origin of the Bible?
"For prophecy never had its origin in the will of man, but men spoke from God as they were carried along by the Holy Spirit." *2 Peter 1:21*

"All Scripture is God-breathed and is useful for teaching, rebuking, correcting and training in righteousness." *2 Timothy 3:16*

Who does the Bible introduce us to?
"In the past God spoke to our forefathers through the prophets at many times and in various ways, but in these last days he has spoken to us by his Son, whom he appointed heir of all things, and through whom he made the universe." *Hebrews 1:1-2*

Why was the Old Testament written?
"For everything that was written in the past was written to teach us, so that through endurance and the encouragement of the Scriptures we might have hope." *Romans 15:4*

What can the Bible do for us?
"The holy scriptures ... are able to make you wise for salvation through faith in Christ Jesus." *2 Timothy 3:15*

Can God's commands in the Scriptures ever be changed?
"Do not add to what I command you and do not subtract from it, but keep the commands of the LORD your God that I gave you." *Deuteronomy 4:2*

Whom did Jesus say would be blessed?
"Blessed ... are those who hear the word of God and obey it." *Luke 11:28*